THE CONSTELLATION COLLECTION

THE LITTLE DIPPER

Joseph Stanley

PowerKiDS
press™

New York

Published in 2016 by The Rosen Publishing Group, Inc.
29 East 21st Street, New York, NY 10010

First Edition

Editor: Katie Kawa
Book Design: Katelyn Heinle

Photo Credits: Cover Yganko/Shutterstock.com; back cover, p. 1 nienora/Shutterstock.com; p. 5 Hollygraphic/Shutterstock.com; p. 7 angelinast/Shutterstock.com; p. 8 AlexanderZam/Shutterstock.com; p. 9 David Nunuk/All Canada Photos/Getty Images; p. 11 Image Work/amanaimagesRF/Getty Images; p. 12 John A Davis/Shutterstock.com; p. 13 PlanilAstro/Shutterstock.com; pp. 15, 17 Babak Tafreshi/National Geographic/Getty Images; p. 16 Scorpp/Shutterstock.com; p. 19 angelinast/Thinkstock.com; p. 21 Valerio Pardi/Shutterstock.com; p. 22 Steve Cole/Photographer's Choice/Getty Images.

Library of Congress Cataloging-in-Publication Data

Stanley, Joseph, author.
The Little Dipper / Joseph Stanley.
    pages cm. — (The constellation collection)
Includes bibliographical references and index.
ISBN 978-1-4994-0939-0 (pbk.)
ISBN 978-1-4994-0961-1 (6 pack)
ISBN 978-1-4994-1004-4 (library binding)
1. Constellations—Juvenile literature. 2. Polestar—Juvenile literature. 3. Ursa Minor—Juvenile literature. I. Title.
QB801.7.S723 2016
523.8—dc23
                        2015014826

Manufactured in the United States of America

CPSIA Compliance Information: Batch #WS15PK: For Further Information contact Rosen Publishing, New York, New York at 1-800-237-9932

CONTENTS

WHAT'S AN ASTERISM?

The night sky is filled with stars that form the shapes of people, objects, and animals. Astronomers—people who study stars and other bodies in space—call 88 of those star formations constellations. Every constellation has a name based on its shape.

Other star formations are smaller, and some are even found within constellations. These smaller star formations are called asterisms. One of the most famous asterisms is the Little Dipper. It's part of a larger constellation named Ursa Minor, or the Little Bear. The Little Dipper is made up of seven stars. Four stars form its bowl, and three form its handle.

THE LITTLE DIPPER IS NAMED AFTER ITS SHAPE, WHICH MANY PEOPLE THROUGHOUT HISTORY SAW AS A SPOON USED TO DIP INTO WATER FOR DRINKING.

POLARIS

STAR STORY

The bright star at the end of
the Little Dipper's handle is
Polaris, which is also known
as the North Star.

TWO DIPPERS

The Little Dipper isn't the only dipper in the sky. The Big Dipper is an asterism in the constellation Ursa Major, or the Great Bear. Both asterisms form the shape of a drinking spoon with a bowl and a handle. Both are also made up of seven stars.

The Big Dipper is easier to find in the sky than the Little Dipper because it's made up of brighter stars. In fact, two of the stars that make up the bowl of the Big Dipper can be used to find the Little Dipper.

STAR STORY
Because the stars that make up most of the Little Dipper aren't very bright, this asterism is best seen away from city lights that cause light pollution, which makes it hard to see any stars.

LITTLE DIPPER

BIG DIPPER

FINDING THE BIG DIPPER FIRST IS THE EASIEST WAY TO FIND THE LITTLE DIPPER.

THE POINTER STARS

Once you find the Big Dipper in the sky, look for the two stars that make up the outer edge of its bowl. These stars are named Merak and Dubhe, and they're also called the pointer stars. That's because they point to Polaris.

NO MATTER WHICH WAY THE LITTLE DIPPER AND THE BIG DIPPER ARE TURNED IN THE SKY, MERAK AND DUBHE ALWAYS POINT THE WAY TO THE NORTH STAR.

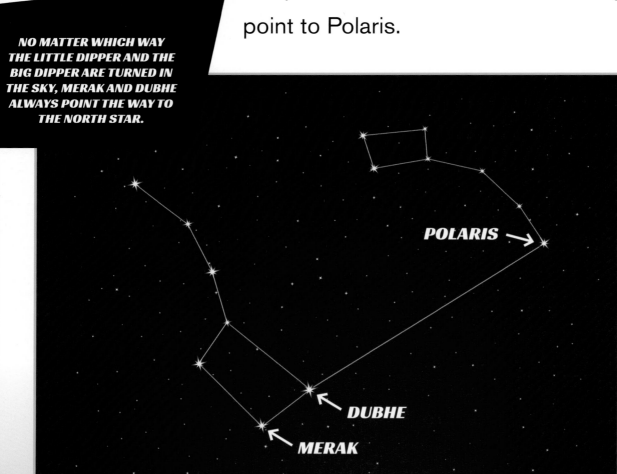

POLARIS →

DUBHE

MERAK

You can draw an imaginary line from Merak and Dubhe to Polaris. The North Star is at the end of the Little Dipper's handle, so Merak and Dubhe point the way to the Little Dipper. Dubhe is the second-brightest star in the Big Dipper. It's also the star in the Big Dipper closest to Polaris, which makes it easy to find.

STAR STORY

Merak and Dubhe got their names from the Arabic language, which was spoken by ancient astronomers from the Middle East. "Merak" means "the **loins**" of the Ursa Major constellation, and "Dubhe" comes from a phrase that refers to the back of the Great Bear.

BIG BEAR, LITTLE BEAR

Ancient people told many **myths** to explain how the shapes of people and animals ended up in the stars. The ancient Greeks had a myth that explained both the Ursa Major and the Ursa Minor constellations.

When Zeus, who was the king of the Greek gods, fell in love with a **nymph** named Callisto, his wife Hera turned Callisto into a bear. Many hunters chased Callisto, including her son Arcas. Before Arcas could kill Callisto, Zeus turned Arcas into a bear to keep him from killing his mother. Then, he also pulled Arcas into the sky, where he became Ursa Minor.

STAR STORY

The handle of the Little Dipper makes up the long tail of Ursa Minor. The Greeks explained this long tail by saying Zeus **stretched** the tail of Arcas when he pulled the bear into the sky.

POLARIS, THE POLESTAR

Polaris is much more than just the star at the end of the Little Dipper's handle and Ursa Minor's tail. It's one of the most important stars in the sky! Polaris is the brightest star in the sky that sits over the North Pole. This is why it's also known as a polestar. If you drew a line straight down from Polaris, it would run almost directly through the North Pole.

Polaris's placement above the North Pole is important because it helps people find their way. If you move toward Polaris, you always know you're heading north.

STAR STORY
Polaris is Earth's northern polestar. Its southern polestar is named Polaris Australis, and it's located almost directly over the South Pole in the Southern **Hemisphere**.

PEOPLE HAVE BEEN USING POLARIS TO NAVIGATE, OR FIND THEIR WAY, FOR THOUSANDS OF YEARS.

CHANGING POLESTARS

Polaris hasn't always been Earth's northern polestar, and it won't always be a polestar. This is because Earth's poles have pointed toward different stars throughout history. As Earth spins on its **axis**, it wobbles like a spinning top. This means that the North Pole isn't always going to be lined up with Polaris like it is right now.

Thousands of years ago, during the time of the ancient Egyptians, a star named Thuban was Earth's northern polestar. Astronomers believe that around 12,000 years from now, a star named Vega will shine above the North Pole instead of Polaris.

STAR STORY
Astronomers believe Vega is currently the fifth-brightest star in the entire sky!

VEGA

SOMEDAY, VEGA, WHICH IS SHOWN HERE, WILL BECOME EARTH'S NORTHERN POLESTAR, AND POLARIS WILL NO LONGER POINT DIRECTLY TO THE NORTH POLE.

NAVIGATING BY STARLIGHT

Polestars have always played an important part in navigation. Travelers have used the stars to navigate on land and sea. Sailors often found their way at night using Polaris to guide them. When sailors measured how far Polaris was above the horizon, they knew how far they were above Earth's **equator**.

Polaris can also help travelers move in the right direction. If they're moving toward Polaris, they're moving north. East is to their right, and west is to their left. If they move backward from Polaris, they're moving south. This never changes, so it's easy to use Polaris as a guide.

STAR STORY

Sailors used tools called sextants to measure the **distance** between a star, such as Polaris, and the horizon. The horizon is the line where the sky seems to meet land or water.

THE LITTLE DIPPER IS ONE OF THE MOST USEFUL STAR FORMATIONS FOR NAVIGATORS BECAUSE THIS ASTERISM IS WHERE POLARIS IS FOUND.

THE GUARDIANS OF THE POLE

During the time of the ancient Greeks, two other stars in the Little Dipper served as polestars. Kochab and Pherkad were closer to the North Pole than Polaris from 1500 BC to AD 500 because of the wobbling of Earth on its axis. These two stars make up the outer edge of the bowl of the Little Dipper.

Polaris is the brightest star in this asterism. Kochab is only slightly fainter than Polaris. Pherkad is the third-brightest star in the Little Dipper. The other stars in this asterism are much harder to see.

STAR STORY

Kochab and Pherkad are sometimes called the Guardians of the Pole.

POLARIS

THE LITTLE DIPPER CAN
BE SEEN IN THE SKY ALL
YEAR IN THE NORTHERN
HEMISPHERE.

KOCHAB

PHERKAD

19

MEASURING MAGNITUDE

Astronomers know Polaris is the brightest star in the Little Dipper, but how do they measure a star's brightness? Star brightness is measured in magnitude. This kind of measurement is a scale. The higher the star's number is on the scale, the fainter the star is. Stars that have a magnitude of 1, or stars of the first magnitude, are very bright.

Polaris has a magnitude of 2. The faintest star in the Little Dipper has a magnitude of 5. Stars of the fifth magnitude can only be seen by people's eyes on very clear nights away from all man-made lights.

STAR STORY

Kochab has a magnitude of 2.08. Pherkad's magnitude is 3.05.

SPACE OBJECTS, SUCH AS STARS, WITH HIGHER MAGNITUDES ARE SEEN MORE EASILY USING TELESCOPES. A TELESCOPE IS A TOOL USED TO MAKE OBJECTS THAT ARE FAR AWAY APPEAR LARGER AND CLEARER.

LOOKING FOR THE LITTLE DIPPER

The Little Dipper has been one of the most helpful star formations for thousands of years because it's been home to polestars, including Kochab, Pherkad, and now Polaris. Sailors and other travelers used the Little Dipper to find their way in the darkness long before more advanced navigation tools were invented.

If you want to see the Little Dipper for yourself, take an adult with you to a place away from city lights on a clear night. It still might be hard to see the whole asterism, but you should be able to spot Polaris very easily.

GLOSSARY

axis: The imaginary straight line that something, such as Earth, turns around.

distance: The space between two points.

equator: An imaginary circle dividing the surface of a body into two equal parts. Earth's equator divides the planet into the Northern and the Southern Hemispheres.

hemisphere: Half of Earth.

loin: An area on the back and sides of an animal's body near the tail.

myth: A story told in ancient cultures to explain a practice, belief, or part of nature.

nymph: A spirit in the shape of a young woman.

stretch: To pull tightly in a way that makes something longer.

INDEX

WEBSITES

Due to the changing nature of Internet links, PowerKids Press has developed an online list of websites related to the subject of this book. This site is updated regularly. Please use this link to access the list: www.powerkidslinks.com/tcc/tld